EUROPEAN POEMS &

Qu'en dis-tu, voyageur, des pays et des gares?
—Paul Verlaine

American River College Library
4700 College Oak Drive
Sacramento, CA 95841

Books by Lawrence Ferlinghetti

LAWRENCE FERLINGHETTI

EUROPEAN POEMS
& TRANSITIONS

OVER ALL THE
OBSCENE BOUNDARIES

A NEW DIRECTIONS BOOK

Copyright © 1980, 1981, 1982, 1983, 1984, 1988 by Lawrence Ferlinghetti

All rights reserved. Except for brief passages quoted in a newspaper, magazine, radio, or television review, no part of this book may be reproduced in any form or by any means, electronic or mechanical, including photocopying and recording, or by any information storage and retrieval system, without permission in writing from the Publisher.

ACKNOWLEDGMENTS
"Fable of the So-called Birds" and earlier versions of "Paris Transformations" and "Canti Romani" were published by New Directions in 1981 in a signed, limited edition.
Grateful acknowledgment is made to the editors and publishers of the following journals in which some of these poems first appeared: *Appeal to Reason, The Baltimore Sun, The City Paper, Combat* (Paris), *Evergreen Review, Exquisite Corpse, Frank, New Directions in Prose & Poetry 41, Pearl, Poet News, San Francisco Chronicle,* and *Sprache im Technischen Zeitalter* (Germany).
The epigram for "The History of the World: A TV Docu-drama" is from *Aphorisms* by Antonio Porchia, used by permission of City Lights Books.

Manufactured in the United States of America
New Directions Books are printed on acid-free paper.
First published clothbound and as New Directions Paperbook 582 in 1984 under the title *Over All the Obscene Boundaries*. Paperbook reprinted in 1988 as *European Poems & Transitions*.
Published simultaneously in Canada by Penguin Books Canada Ltd.

Library of Congress Cataloging-in-Publication Data
Ferlinghetti, Lawrence.
European poem & transitions : over all the obscene boundaries.
Rev. ed. of: Over all the obscene boundaries. c1984.
Includes index.
I. Ferlinghetti, Lawrence. Over all the obscene boundaries.
II. Title. III. Title: European poems and transitions.
PS3511.E55709 1988   811'.54   88-1789
ISBN 0-8112-1084-7 (pbk.)

New Directions Books are published for James Laughlin
by New Directions Publishing Corporation
80 Eighth Avenue, New York 10011

THIRD PRINTING

CONTENTS

PARIS TRANSFORMATIONS

1.

Clay somnambule returned
                    after many years away

        walking and walking
                    through once-loved Paris
        Gare du Nord to Montparnasse
            Rue de la Roquette and Place Voltaire
                Place Léon Blum and Père Lachaise
                    Les Halles and Tour St. Jacques
                        Saint Sulpice and Cherche Midi
                        (where I searched my Noon)

Strode through the streets
                thirsty and sad
                            (yet exultant!)
                carrying nothing
                            but youth

Now the closed bus carries me
                    past the place I lay on the quai

The map of Paris
                stamped upon my brainpan

2.

I left my memory in hock
on the rooftops of Paris
where the grey light of Paris lays
like the shadow at the back of old mirrors
And the sky a grey scrim behind the river
where at noon the sun bursts through
with a golden stroke,
a scimitar ablaze,
tearing the veil of days.

3.

That lovely balcony is gone
                in the Impasse Danton
        and with it the lady
                with the scales
        who sat there once
                (the blind one in the classic frieze)
Now an ounce of memory
                moves these scales in a breeze
I feel the weight of her breast
                against me pressed

But she was young then
                and wore no blindfold
        (Blind maiden
                not blind in love!)
I hold her hand still
                like a limp white glove

In the closed dark bedroom
with the heavy silk drapes
she throws open
the huge French doors
And the dry white wine of dawn
floods in

The white sun of Paris
softens sidewalks
sketches white shadows on skylights
traps a black cat
on a distant balcony

And the whole city sleeping drifts
through white space
like a lost dirigible
unconscious of
the immense mystery

6.

Place Saint Sulpice
     le soir
Lady in a coal-shovel hat
       crosses the street
Dupré's organ music
      follows her from the church
A black poodle
     also follows her
        like a shadow
The leaves of the plane trees quiver
       as if expecting rain
A fat dame in a plain apron
      stands at the bar with a crutch
   at the back of the *Café de la Mairie*
         du Sixième
    and eats a *Croque-Monsieur*
    with her
      false teeth
     her face
       fallen out of Goya
A priest comes out and closes
       the iron gate of the church
Six minutes later he cycles past
     with flowers on the back
       of his old clunker
The dusk descends
The people all disappear
       into doorways
The sidewalks like flat escalators
     roll away into the night
Trees, fountains, statues,
      the café and the church itself
   melt into total darkness

As still somewhere
          a bell tolls
                    the mad idea
     of a Christian society

The big barges push through
under the Pont Mirabeau.
A huge sculptured mermaid
with golden torch
looks down upon them.
A barge man in black beret
looks up
the same way he looked up
at the last bridge
at the first Statue of Liberty
with eyes like worn pennies.

Et sous le Pont Mirabeau
coule la liberté.

A homesick jade elephant
with eyes half-closed
sits by the Seine
in the lotus position
dreaming of the Nile

He puts his trunk in the river
and siphons up the sound
of October and autos
and the smell of distant spring
which is Paris echoing
some lost life
of wonder and laughter
in which Myrna Loy might appear
with Ramon Novarro singing to her
an Arabian Love Song
floating down the river
in a felucca

He's walking about
in his Egyptian pajamas.
Through the side streets of Paris
the little narrow alleys
he's leading his humpy camel.
He has a halo on his head
which will not go away
as in Marcel Aymé.
The camel will not fit through
some of the crooked alleys.
It is like trying to pull him through
the eye of a rusty needle.
Also the halo gets stuck
in the low branches of trees.
Nevertheless he must cross Paris
with his camel and his halo.
Once in a while a sniper on a rooftop
takes a shot at him.
But the bullets bounce off his halo
like pinballs in a slot machine.
When they finally reach
the far end of town
they lie down together
the camel and the man with the halo
in the Egyptian pajamas.
But they cannot sleep or make love.
The camel's hump and the halo
always get in the way.
Suddenly they are seized
with uncontrollable laughter
And they roll around together on the ground
convulsed with the thought
of their comic situation on earth.

Tristes banlieues,
saisons, châteaux,
et toutes ces tristesses
de la Ligne de Sceaux.
But then again the things that still amaze
And autumn capitols
their avenues of leaves ablaze
avec leurs douces fugues,
tristes banlieues,
saisons, châteaux,
et toutes ses tristes joies
qui ont lieu
au coeur brisé.

11.

My hand was not mine
It wandered over my body all night
looking for a place to rest
Sartre's nausea filled my being
A chestnut branch
reached in the window
and scratched my heart
A tired cicada
started taking off its skin
Only the singing
of a distant swan
saved me from swooning away
A huge bumblebee flew in
and awarded me a golden sting
I fell over sideways
my tongue in a sling

I meant to pick a paper poppy
from the fields of Normandy
the coquelicots of Monet
in my memory
and memory a mix of blooms
unpicked in rime
a mix of wings
untied in time
So that a coquelicot
becomes an orange sun
when day is
almost done
And the blind sphinx of life
eats my mind

For years I never thought of death.
Now the breath
of the eternal harlequin
makes me look up
as if a defrocked Someone were there
who might make me into an angel
playing piano on a riverboat.

RETURNING TO PARIS WITH PISSARRO

I am in a painting by Camille Pissarro
Place du Théâtre Français
Paris in the Rain 1898
only it is not 1898
It is 1948
a slight juggling of numbers
and no horse carriages
but the same eternal feeling
sad and elated
walking in Paris in the rain
I can feel it coming through
the French canvas
the light rain falling
out of the pearl skies
the Opera a deep pearl
in the far distance
of the Avenue de l'Opéra
And the domed roofs of the Théâtre Français
the stricken winter trees
the smell of Gaulois at the Metro entrance
(which doesn't exist yet in the picture)
the fountain in front of the Théâtre
still spouting in the rain
And the dark chimneys
above the wet mansard roofs
above the fifth floor running balconies
and the grey awnings along the Avenue
dark figures under umbrellas
two by two
or clustered at corners
The grey Paris light
lies on the great buildings

like a light gauze veil
the lucent light
glimmers on the wet paving
on the sidewalks under the trees
You can almost hear
the clop-clop of horses
drawing the fiacres
The rain has let up
It seems about to clear
the veil to be torn away
pearl about to open
in the sky of 1948—
I am *twenty*-eight
with new eyes alight
returning to Paris with Pissarro
from the New World

LA DAME AUX CAMELIAS

(*from an old movie*)

After ringing the bell for some time and no answer
he entered the tall hallway of that elegant
French apartment
having a rendezvous for lunch and expecting someone
to come forward from an inner room and greet him
(a table set with wine in the background)
But a faint low voice came from behind
a closed door
'In here,' the voice said, 'In here'
and as he entered the darkened room
he could see her lying under the camelia covers
as she held out her hand saying, 'Here—
I am here—'
as he took her hand and took her face
in his hands and kissed her closed eyes and
kissed them once again and she
did not open them and the
light slanted through
the closed shutters and he
could see the light on her blue eye–shadow and
there was nothing to do but kiss
her hands and eyes and he
did so for a long time
and there still was no one else and
nothing living except
the two of them there although
the earth still turned and he
had a feeling of floating as
on a still pool
the camelias
were floating

in the dark pool of
their lives in that shaded room where
she lay saying over and over
'It's you It's you' and he
was thinking that if he
could only piece together the fragments of
that shuttered Paris light he
might be able to
reassemble the torn pieces of
their lives into
one coherent
clear photo which
someday somehow he
might possibly
decipher

A DARK PORTRAIT

She always said '*tu*' in such a way

as if she wanted to sleep with you

or had just had

     a most passionate

          orgasm

And she *tutoyé*d everyone

But she

     was really like Nora in *Nightwood*

  long-gaited and restless as a mare

and coursed the cafés

     through revolving doors and nights

  looking for the lover

     who would never satisfy her

And when she grew old

     slept among horses

SEEING A WOMAN AS IN A PAINTING
BY BERTHE MORISOT

Ah *tes cuisses*
as in an hour-glass
(through which all flesh flows)
at the cafe table now
you are living you are breathing
your bosom stirs
so slightly so lightly
belle plante bell jar
unaware of your self
full
of breath and life
not yet
awakened
I feel your breath so light
across the loud cafe
dear distant one
the time will come
or will not come
when we shall know
why we live and why we love
the time will come
or will not come
when you'll awake
from your deep dream of youth
the time will come or will not come
when we shall know
why all things pass
through the hour-glass
and why we now are here
in the late morning
listening to a juke-box Puccini

and looking away from each other
as if we did not know the music
as if we did not know the melody

WOMEN IN ROOMS

Seeing women in small rooms
is not the same as
being with women anywhere else
It is something about
the womb of the affair
I look across the night courtyard
and see through the curtains
an intimate interior
Two women move about in it
slowly
gravely
lightly
their gestures at once
transparent and profound
I am a voyeur of their
erotic
ordinary lives
I am inside their lives
inside their bodies
inside their eyes
where lies the mystery—

Of a sudden
the light goes out
like a candle blown
And they with it
like moths blown out
onto a dark landscape

CAFÉ NOTRE DAME

A sort of sexual trauma
has this couple in its thrall
He is holding both her hands
in both his hands
She is kissing his hands
They are looking
in each other's eyes
Up close
She has a fur coat
made of a hundred running rabbits
He
is wearing a formal
dark coat and dove grey trousers
Now they are inspecting the palms
of each other's hands
as if they were maps of Paris
or of the world
as if they were looking for the Metro
that would take them together
through subterranean ways
through the 'stations of desire'
to love's final terminals
at the ports of the city of light
It is a terminal case
But they are losing themselves
in the crisscrossing lines
of their intertwined palms
their head-lines and their heart-lines
their fate-lines and life-lines
illegibly entangled
in the *mons veneris*
of their passion

MAKING LOVE IN POETRY

(After Breton)

In a war where every second counts
Time drops to the ground
like a shadow from a tree
under which we lie
in a wood boat built from it
by an unknown carpenter beyond the sea
upon which peach pits float
fired by a gunner who has run out of ammunition
for a cannon whose muzzle bites heartshaped holes
out of the horizon of our flesh
stunned in sun and baffled into silence
between the act of sex
and the act of poetry
blissed-out in the darkening air
at the moment of loving and coming
there is no glimpsing of
the misery of the world

BACH & MOZART IN
SAINT-JULIEN-LE-PAUVRE

I n this eternal grotto
crenelated cave
we *bêtes civilisées*
sit and listen to
this *musique celeste*
this divine musick
clavecin et violon
a divine insanity
a sweetness and a glory
such loveliness and loneliness
in the high sound of it
compounded in the art of it
Mozart's heart
stirring in it
And now the beatitudes of Bach
in chromatic fugue
the *violon baroque*
like a fine wood boat
carried away on the wild waters
on the wild stream of the fugue
dancing ecstatic now
in the shoals of that music
to eddy away at last
into the night gardens of
Julien-le-pauvre
and into the night sky
with its ecstatic geometries
and the Bacchic night-music
of the spheres

DARKNESS, CHEZ GEORGE WHITMAN

Sometime toward four A.M.
softly on the stone rooftops
softly on the old skylights
I could hear the separate drops
falling like soft pellets

When the rain at last gave up
an owl somewhere
started up its glum complaint
and when a cat got its tongue
gave a croak and rolled over

which caused a single bird to fly over
from the gardens of *Julien-le-pauvre*
and start a complicated threnody
a sweet story a sad story
an oh-so-melancholy story
to some old melody

Then back it flew
into some oubliette
leaving only silence to forget
and more silence
with its own tale to tell
of paradise and hell

as I lay there waiting
for the next wing of darkness
to swoop down on me

THE ANGRY GOD

Paris Rue de la Bûcherie
six heures du matin
the iron bell strikes through the stone streets
a bloody murderer of sleep and sin
at six in the morning
the monster knocks me awake
Some mad priest
bludgeoning the rusty bell
in its great stone tower
Saint-Julien-le-pauvre or Saint-Séverin
or Quasimodo maybe
on Notre Dame
The mad man is flailing at it
with his iron truncheon
in his rusty robes
insistent
implacable
a hollow thumping an urgent clanging
through the bent streets at dawn
The earth shakes
like an old dog awaking
Dies irae! Sin and Salvation!
Death grinds its dusty teeth
There is still an angry god somewhere
giving us Hell

UNDER THE BRIDGES

U*n 'coup de Sirocco'*

soufflait sur moi

Pigeons make me flutter

I awake and see the Seine

high in its banks

after Spring rains

The ochre water

courses by

flushing through Paris

its dark country sediments

In the dark dawn

I heard the ocean roar far off

Sea stirred in me

as now the current floods around

Ile Saint-Louis

as around a floating memory

Gulls flutter over it

as above a ship adrift inside of me

Et sous les ponts de Paris

coule ma vie

VOIX GLAUQUE

Now that bird of life
                   with its *bouche avare*
          makes as if to devour us

Except it cannot do it
              as long as we keep singing
                      and making love
           for this sets up vibrations
                   in its throat
           which make it impossible
                      to swallow us

It is the dead bird
             in the heart
                  that kills us

As on this Sunday afternoon
                   sky grey over Les Halles
      from the fifth floor balcony
            I see stick figures lost below
                 the mute singers and the walking dead
       And one pigeon walks about silent
             and one or two
                   fly through the heavy air
  It does not matter that the sky
                  is made of lead
          or that no bells toll
                    anywhere

Inside ourselves is the song
                as in an *oboe d'amore*
It sounds in us so distantly

                    so insistently
          a distant singing
                         a far crying
          so faintly echoing—
                         glaucous voice
                         beyond our little turning world
It is life itself singing
               its exultant harmonies
          and stretching over us
                    its darkling wings

HE WITH THE BEATING WINGS

The lark has no tree
                    the crow no roost
        the owl no setting place
                    the nightingale
                                no certain song
And he with the beating wings
                    no place to light
                                in the neon dawn
                    his tongue too long ago
                                retuned
            by those ornithologists
                                the state has hired
                to make sure
                    the bird population of the world
                remains stable
                                and pinioned
    There is no need
                to clip its claws
    Its tongue will do
                Tether the tongue
        and all falls fallow
                The wild seed drops
                        into nothingness
    Tether the tongue
                and all falls
                        into silence
        a condition ever desired
                            by tyrants
                not least of which is
                            the great state
            with its benevolent birdwatchers
                        with their nets and binoculars

32

watching out for
                    the wild one
          He that bears Eros
                          like a fainting body
              He that bears
                          the gold bough
          He
              with the beating wings

L'OCCUPATION OBSÉDÉE

Assis sur la terrasse Café Saint-Séverin
J'entends des voix allemandes de chaque côté
Et la voix américaine
le Latin de nos jours
Avec son empire qui roule toujours
C'est toujours Normandie 1944
Avec ses voix américaines et ses voix allemandes
Suis toujours en train de débarquer!
Je lis toujours *Le Canard Enchaîné*
Je lis *Libération* toujours
Je vois encore l'oiseau délabré
J'entends encore la voix criante
La voix palpitante
de l'accordéon
dans le métro
l'hiver 1944
Où je sens encore
les Gauloises Jaunes
Suis toujours occupé
occupé des rêves-pensées
Qui me disent que la vie toujours
est noble et tragique
et les barques d'amour toujours
se brisent sur les côtes
de la vie de tous-les-jours
de la vie hebdomadairienne
du *Monde Hebdomadaire*
où je lis encore
qu'il y a toujours la Résistance
qu'on va contrôler bien sur
Oui, la Résistance toujours
contre l'état monstre
contre les chaines sur l'oiseau

O lost gardens
Forgotten fountains
Tournesols détournés
Cannabis caché
L'herbe *sin semilla*
Oiseau frappé
bouche bouclée
Fraternité.

MONSIEUR NICOLAS

Monsieur Nicolas est arrivé
chez nous ce matin
Ce n'est pas tous les jours
que Monsieur Nicolas arrive
Nouveau Christ de la Rue Les Halles
Il n'apporte pas de vin
Il monte de l'eau des montagnes
Comme le Christ il s'est leve
de très bonne heure
et il arrive avec de l'eau fraiche
Alors Monsieur Nicolas m'apparut
exactement comme je l'imaginais
durant toutes ces années
Il portait un grand tablier noir
et des souliers noirs
trop grands pour lui
Et il avait une petite moustache noire
et des yeux très noirs
J'étais au pieu
mais il insistait
il sonnait la sonnette
comme la trompette du jugement dernier
Je pensais qu'il se decouragerait
et qu'enfin il partirait
Mais après dix minutes de sonnerie
il ne part pas il reste
il sonne il crie enfin
Nicolas! Nicolas!
Enfin je me suis levé et enfin
j'ai ouvert la porte
Voilà Monsieur Nicolas
comme le Père Saint Nicolas

en train de casser sa croûte
assis sur les marches de l'escalier
Il mangeait son croque-monsieur
et il boit son eau
C'est comme ça avec Monsieur Nicolas
Si on répond pas
à son appel
on attend
on descend pas du Mont
on ne part pas
on casse la croûte
et on attend
parce que
C'est certain
C'est fixé
C'est ordonné
qu'un jour
des gens auront tous
une très grande soif
la plus grande soif
la soif de vivre toujours
la soif de l'éternité même
Et c'est à ce moment-là
que Monsieur Nicolas gagne
comme le Christ

AMANT DES GARES

Suis amant des gares
amateur des gares
les gares de toutes sortes
n'importe où
à cause de ma très grande soif
de gens et de la vie des gens
les foules dans les gares
et les solitaires dans les foules
J'ai fait mon bac
dans la Rue du Bac
mais c'est dans les gares
où j'ai fait mon doctorat
mon doctorat de vie
C'est les gares qui m'avalent
surtout si j'attends quelqu'un
ou quelqu'une
sur le quai d'une gare
quelqu'un pour qui j'ai si faim
pour qui j'ai si soif
et qui a envie de moi
et que j'attends toujours
J'attends toujours ceux qui m'attendent
comme tout le monde
avec cette enorme soif
cette enorme faim
de tout manger tout boire
comme des animaux affamés
qui mangent tout
dans la grande beuverie de la vie
où le soleil viendra un jour
pour bouffer tout ça

FINISTÈRE

(from an old movie)

Finistère!
Comme ce nom réverbère
dans la mémoire
de cet homme
de cet ancien marin
en Finistère
Ca me fait frissoner du coeur—
Finistère!
C'est encore l'hiver
C'est toujours la guerre de quarante-quatre
C'est toujours toutes les guerres
les guerres du temps qui mangent tout
Le temps qui a tué tout
en Finistère
cette année là—
tu es toujours là avec tes fleurs
dans les bras
sur le quai en Finistère
C'était déjà tard
tu prenais un bateau
du Finistère
pour aller loin n'importe où
C'est comme ça que ça s'est passé
Oui c'est arrivé comme ça
Le vent souffle toujours
sur les côtes sauvages
du Finistère
Ce vent sauvage qui a soufflé
sur toi et sur moi
et sur les voiles de ce bateau

Adieu
oui Adieu
Ah oui je sais C'est vachement banal
Le vent soufflait Adieu Adieu
et nous l'avons entendu
nous l'avons accepté
Adieu Adieu c'est tout
Ton bateau est parti
de l'embarcadère
Ah oui je sais C'est vachement banal
le bateau est disparu
dans la brume du Finistère
et je suis resté debout
en Finistère
avec tes fleurs
(c'était de la lavande
qui ne fanne jamais)
sur le quai des brumes
de ma vie affamée

OISEAU DÉLABRÉ

Oiseau délabré

et onirique

avec ta gueule si lyrique

si satirique

Ah oui je te connais toujours

surtout quand tu te dresse sur moi

en remuant ton aile délabrée

en criant de ta voix si insensée

si dechirée

(mais toujours passionante

délirante

et énigme)

TRISTE CORBIÈRE

A clamor of gulls
outside the French windows
above the tidepools
in the stone harbor
in Roscoff Brittany
in the Hotel des Bains
top floor under the eaves
I look down and see
the damned poet
Tristan Corbière
walking along the quai
in this stone town
with its fishscale skies
where a street is named after him
a small dark stone street
twisting to the sea
Even at this distance
I see the black crow's feet
on his head
where a crow gripped him
and tried to fly away with him
Triste Corbière
with your countenance of night
Now a black gull
flies away with a fish
in the dark daylight
And a black crow watches
from a great height
an ebony crow
a huge crow
made of nothing but night
Only his feet are red

from holding the head of the poet
red with the blood of the poet
with his countenance of night

MORLAIX: INTO THE FUTURE
WITH NEIL YOUNG

At the Café de la Terrasse
I've given myself up
to the essence of things
trying to tune in on
what's going on here
if anything
Young French would-be punk-rock stars
listening to American westerns on the juke
trying to figure out
how to get out of town
Son of the local pork butcher
in leather pants and dark glasses
snaps his fingers to the beat
figuring out nothing
A slight wind has come up
with the smell of roast chestnuts
in this little town of Morlaix
with its stone aqueduct high-over
The town bandstand empty
The chestnut trees around it
waving their lush leaves
Nothing else moves It's the provinces
deep summer
Neil Young comes on the juke
You can almost see his Stetson
and the hole in his guitar
An old nag clops around a corner
into the Place de la Mairie
Suddenly following the horse
an amazing cavalcade appears
a troupe of masked mummers

to the sound of a flute and a small tambour
beaten with a stick
The mystery behind their masks
must remain a mystery
as if it were life itself
Otherwise these would-be escapees
might not run off with this travelling show of life
in their hot youth and heat
over the hill through time and dangers
to the crystal canyons
and the Motel of Lost Companions
with heated pool and waterbeds
full of shining strangers

THE GENERALS—A NAIVE DREAM

The modern military bus
sits in the rain in Paris
Place du Trocadero
in front of the monument to the war dead
the frieze of figures frozen
À NOS HEROS—À NOS MORTS
The empty khaki-colored bus
sits there in the rain
as through the trees we see
Marshall Foch on his bronze horse
and the chestnut trees are turning yellow
on the Avenue of President Wilson
where General George Washington
sits on his high horse
with sword upraised in the rain
when all of a sudden
the two generals wheel about
on their great metal steeds
and gallop toward each other
Washington throws his sword
over the treetops
and it falls in a field in Normandy
where it turns into a ploughshare
and Marshall Foch throws his little pistol
into the Musée de Guerre Moderne
The two generals are still galloping
toward each other
Now only the military bus separates them
They both dismount
and advance toward each other
like unhorsed medieval knights
The American general takes a neutron bomb

out of his hip pocket
and dismantles it
The French general kisses the American general
on both cheeks
His Marshall Foch moustache comes off
and remains on the cheek of the American
The acid rain stops falling
Il fait beau

PLAN DU CENTRE DE PARIS
À VOL D'OISEAU

Flying away to Milan
I look down and back at Paris
(as in that famous map
seen by a bird in flight)
and think of Allen yesterday
saying it was all 'solidified nostalgia'—
houses monuments and streets
bare trees and parks down there
fixed in time (and the time is forever)
exactly where we left them years ago
our bodies passed through them
as through a transparent scrim
Early versions of ourselves
transmuted now
two decades later
And was that myself
standing on that far corner
Place Saint-Sulpice
first arrived in Paris—
seabag slung—
(fancying myself some seaborn Conrad
carrying Coleridge's albatross?)
or was that myself walking
through the Tuileries in early snow?
And here Danton met Robespierre
(both later to descend into earth
through that Metro entrance)
And here Sartre lived with Beauvoir
above the Café Bonaparte
before death
shook them apart

(The myth goes on)
And here in the Luxembourg
I sat by a balustrade
in a rented iron chair
reading Proust and Apollinaire
while the day turned to dust
and a nightwood sprang up around me
Solidified nostalgia indeed—
the smell of Gaulois still hangs in the air
And in the cemetery of Père Lachaise
the great stone tombs still yawn
with the solidified ennui of eternity
And, yes, here I knew such aloneness—
at the corner of another street
the dawn yawned
in some trauma I was living in back then
Paris itself a floating dream
a great stone ship adrift
made of dusk and dawn and darkness—
dumb trauma
of youth!
such wastes of love
such wordless hungers
mute neuroses
yearnings & gropings
fantasies & flame-outs
such endless walking
through the bent streets
such fumbling art
(models drawn with blindfolds)
such highs and sweet inebriations—
I salute you now
dumb inchoate youth
(callow stripling!)
and offer you my left hand
with a slight derisive laugh

HOW CLEAR YOUR VOICE
FROM BELGRADE

Young friend when you rang up
your voice so clear
you might have been downstairs
in this Milan hotel
not across three sets of mountains
and thirty rivers
not across three ideologies
and three languages
not across various curtains
made of heavy metal and static
How clear your voice from Belgrade
I hope mine is that clear
I can almost see your voice
sailing through the Cimabue blue
over the mountains and rivers
a white bird winging its way high over
as in a Magritte painting
flying out of the deep cobalt blue
out of which bombs are made
A great white bird
flying straight over
as the dove might make it after all
over all the obscene boundaries
Your voice so clear
    Bella Katy
      bella Katalina

RISTORANTE VITTORIA, MILAN

Three baldheaded men at the next table
 speaking accented English which is
 native to none of them
Maybe two are Italian and one is from
 Egypt and doesn't know the *bella lingua*
They are discussing deepsea mining
 (One thousand meters down—nodules!)
Perhaps I should report it to the CIA
 (that international terrorist group)
Suspicious discussion in American
 the language of the conquerors—
We are alone in the restaurant
 among the linen-covered tables
 and the huge silver
I decide at length that they are all Italian
 putting me on
 for some perverse reason
I decide to pretend I don't understand
 the strange language they are talking
 maintaining an inscrutable and urbane countenance
 like some debonair expatriot character
 in Henry James
 putting my meat in my mouth
 with the fork in the left hand
 in the Continental manner
 having read an international spy novel
 in which the American fugitive
 gives himself away
 by changing his fork back to his right hand
 before raising it to his mouth
I am seriously pursuing this line of behavior
 as the three men with bald nodules

continue their seemingly serious discussion
about the deep sea
off the coast of Abyssinia
though at any moment we might all
burst out in riotous laughter
at the ludicrous absurdity
of the whole charade

FIRENZE, A LIFETIME LATER

'A cavatina of broken parlando utterances'
   punctuated by sighs
      was the sound of the river Arno passing through
         that Tuscan countryside that evening
            as we lay on a grass bank
               trailing our hands in the ochre waters
      as if we were students again
        just hitchhiked down from Paris
   and as if this dreamt re-enactment
      might have the same ending again
         as that first time we
            returned to the same *pensione*
      and made love in the same *camera*
        to the dark tremolo of the same doves
Only this time
         our lives not shaken
               by our coming

AN AFTERNOON IDYLL

The flowers
        love Caruso
    lifting their
                blue throats
        to his
                high vibrato
    taut stems aquiver
                    like cello strings touched
    Iris lyric
            purple light
        a flight
            out of darkness
    Sun
        in the yellow room
                    turns around
                        two still figures
            on a crimson couch
                        carried away
                in Caruso's seas

SCENE FROM A STREET OPERA

The two young dogs making it
                on the sidewalk in the late sun
        the two big beautiful dogs
                                stuck together
                motionless and mute
                                perfectly still
            the way they get when
                        one has it in the other
            but these two
                        have gotten turned around
                                backwards
                        facing away
                                from each other
                tail to tail
                                and
                they can't move or
                                turn back around
                hung up together
                                And
            the sun is setting and
                            people are passing
                without looking
                        at these two dumb beasts
                just standing there
                            looking blindly looking dumbly
                away from each other
    Naked fuckers
            coupled together in heat
                        in a public place
            (ghetto graffiti
                lewd pornography!)
                        locked in that

55

                    so dumb embrace
While on the Square
                the big bell
                        starts its tolling
        the air
                filled suddenly
                        with a
                                dark fluttering
                of small birds flittering
                        to the very top
                of a huge dark tree
                                setting up
                                a great crying
                        into the last rays
                                of the setting sun
Is it Seville in spring
                when day is done
Is it Carmen and
                her silent lover
                        'I must
                                see you again Carmen
                                The flower you gave me faded'
        The world full-up
                        with creatures coupling
        as here and now
                        these two four-legged beasts
                their fur now
                                suddenly trembling
                        the hind part
                        of one of them
                                now quivering
        While the passersby
                the two-legged ones
                                cannot embrace passing strangers
                                        like dogs

56

And we hurry on alone
>through the end of day
Except for one old Don José
>in an old black
>>felt hat
>who turns around a block away
>>and looks back
>and looks and looks
>>with a long long gaze . . .
'*Ah we were*
>*blind animals back then*
>>*in those dumb days*
>*My dear Carmen*'

THE LIGHT

Couples on the boat to the Isola di Giglio
in the Tuscan archipelago
wrapped up in each other
What does he see in her
and her in him—
He strokes her leg
She loves him
What a look
she lays on him
I   love   you
It's a mystery
It continues
There's an old *pescatore* watching them
He wishes he were him
Obviously he's come a long way
the fisher with his face like Sicily
with his hands like crabs
He would like to haul her in
but his net already has
too many fish in it
He's already hauled it in
too many times
with big old ones and little ones
stuck in the net
his *famiglia*
Still he eyes the Venus on the hook
as if it were his
as if he had caught it
and didn't quite know
what to do with it
It's the eternal mystery
Fat legs she has

but a face from a Greek coin
the light of Greece in it
Ah yes that's it
the light in the eyes
in spite of all
fat legs and dim brain
tuttavia
It's the light that counts
the light that attracts the fish at night

JOHN LENNON IN THE
PORTO SANTO STEFANO

A *trattoria* in the *porto:*
an astonishingly beautiful couple enters
in shorts
He's got a fantastic torso
long hair and a golden headband
She's got long flaxen hair
German hippies maybe
Bourgeois back home
Another couple saunters in and joins them
Dark hair and jeans
Comme ils sont beaux
Not one of them is gay
though he's the most beautiful
He's got such a smile
Some story he's telling
What could it be
Something about John Lennon
lost in a mix of Tuscan and German
Comme elle est belle
with her empty eyes
the Germans very spaced out
the Italians very together
But none of them look very happy
Perhaps it's just youth
I am trying to think of a Lennon line
to sum up the situation
There isn't any
He didn't live long enough to give us
the mad eternal answer

THE MOUTH OF TRUTH

Is this the mouth of truth
in the face of this woman
walking across the *Piazza*
Bocca della Verità
where the great round stone is set up
in the portico of the Church of
Santa Maria in Cosmedin
her little feet taking her
past the Temple of the Virgins
past the Temple of the Phallus
and past the Street of the Misericordia
She has not been kneeling
in any church
She trots along on her too high heels
She has smart rhinestone glasses
and silk pants very well cut
She has a sweet face
spoiled by lipstick
a botched attempt
at something but the truth
She could be the daughter of a shah
but she isn't
She's some secretary
Late at the office
the boss was beastly tonight
Her mouth must have answered
Those rouge lips could cope with
any tongue
She's tough in a way
but not so tough
She has her soft spots
her lower lip

is very sensitive
You can tell there are other soft places
from that
She has her cigarette lit
in her right hand
the same hand she may have put
into the Mouth of Truth
that great round pagan stone
at the mouth of the church
which will bite off your hand
if you're hiding some lie
She did not put her head
into the mouth of the lion
Her left hand has rings
in the wrong places
She doesn't have a boyfriend
this year
but she has her cigarette
You can tell it is a close friend
the way she fondles it
It is a filter tip
She is looking forward
to lying down on her bed
in the dark
in her slip
with the window open
There is a tree outside
In the morning a bird
She is smoking her cigarette
her mouth of truth around the filter
which has filtered out
all but the truth
The truth will come through
the truth will out
the mouth fall open

when she's asleep on her back
by the open window
by the tree with its leaves like lips
the lower lip so sensitive
will quiver
the throat utter some deep sound
the tongue mute messenger
with its speechless truth
To whom will she tell it
in what dream
and what 'dark dove with flickering tongue'
pass below the far horizon
of her longing?

CANTI ROMANI

I

At Kennedy Airport
two nuns swoop by
one carrying the other on her back
                flapping her arms
                        like wings
              weeping and laughing at the same time
        and waving her very white hands
                which flutter
                        like white doves
They settle on her breasts

There is a whir in the air
                  as we fly through it
The nuns spread their wings
                and fly away after us
To Fiumicino
Their landing gears do not retract
and they float about in circles
                looking for a soft landing
Ernest Hemingway looks up and cries
    'Frankly, my dear, I don't give a damn'
The nuns circle about
as a red bird flies by
'As Time Goes By' comes out of a piano
                  in an Algiers café
The nuns land on the piano
Bogart says 'Play it again, Sam'
Sam starts unrolling the nylons
                off the nuns on his piano
It is like a run on a bank

When one starts
                they all run
Pretty soon they are all dancing
Like skaters on a winter pond
                they whirl about
                        disrobing as they whirl

And sin has no sight of them

II

This is how things would seem
from forty thousand feet
Up closer down on earth
we realize that is not how things are at all
Nuns do not fly about so easily
without tethers and feathers
And the landscape is not just checkered
                              black and white
There are infinite gradations of earth
and the gradations overcome you
                    The detail
                        becomes the tragedy
                or the commedia
                        to put it more comically
The picturesque hillock
                        becomes a hazard
                        to the lowered landing gear
The hills in the distance
                    are seen to be greenest
                              for unsuspected reasons

Even as we lie in a darkened room
behind closed shutters by the balcony
in the Hotel Venezia Via Varese
We cannot see the hills from here
when the bells somewhere
suddenly start tolling
and a red bird flies by
where the wolf learned Latin
It must be five o'clock
in Roma Monday afternoon
Some church nearby
is raising the dust with its bells

a great clanging and banging
The towers must be shaking
In a while we shall go out
and flash about the streets
for a quick look in the shaken light
without frightening the natives
The Colosseum is still there
I saw it when we came in today
in the airport bus
                to the Stazione Termini
It was engulfed in a sea of cars
but they still had to go around
I could still hear the gladiators
yelling at their horses
and the cries of the warriors and martyrs
being run through
with spears and long swords
mixed with the cries of taxi drivers
                and tour guides
Some stone general on a horse
          a great casque upon his head
on top of a pedestal
        in the center of a great traffic circle
directing the motorized chariots . . .
The legions thunder by!

III

Dante learning the lingua
at his mother's knee
sees the swallows flying over
A Roman summer plover
flies in from seaward
It is morning on the balcony
over the city
The sun hits the side
                    of the ochre building
It is still sleeping
        its shutters still closed
A few small swallows still fly over
The air is full of light breathing
The city lets out a great sigh
before it starts up for the day
Somewhere some motors start up
A red bird flies over
Another hot day heats up
We sit out on the stone balcony
drinking black coffee from a small cup

IV

At midnight on the next balcony
a naked man standing in the dense dark
smoking and looking down
Across the way a naked lady unaware
comes out and sits upon a chair
They do not see each other
in the curtained air
At dawn they are gone
and thousands of swallows
flicker down
silent, flittering
flickering over the rooftops
It is as if the muted air
were made of the down of their wings
of the sound the hushed sound
of their wings
which none but another bird could hear
It is as if the first light
were made for singing
It is as if Dante were walking
from roof to roof
lightly singing
           a muted melody
lightly humming
           to himself
                a fretted threnody
lightly treading
           the tiled balconies
      the marble terraces
The swallows
           swirl about him
With the dawn they dart away
leaving feathers in his hair

woven like laurel
in the sweet air
so full of our strange life
so bitter yet so passing fair

V

Along the Appian Way
children are playing
imitating marching soldiers and battles
chattering and shrieking like swallows
                                    at evening
There is a thrill in the air
a sound of tiny tin drums
hidden somewhere
                    over the hills
as if there were a fair somewhere
which we were not allowed to approach
a fair militaire
which retreats always beyond us
beyond the horizon
as we advance
waving our colored rags of flags
Furiously
we wave them
imitating marching soldiers and battles
Avànti!
Combàttere! Obbedire!
Lòtta Continua!
Lining the great Way
the crowds cheer
                    waving their ragged rainbows
The dusk is falling
the children disappear
babies rolled away in prams
crowds melted
                    into nothingness
Only the great pines remain
the great still trees
                    the heavy-headed trees

as in a Turner landscape
as a great silence descends
on the windless reaches
And then far away
far off and faint
intermittent
hesitant
heard and unheard
as in Respighi
a slow distant drumming
a distant thrumming
an insistent churning
as of many feet together turning
Along the Appian Way
among the dark pines and shattered shadows
in the dark day
as a red bird flies over
new legions coming
new legions marching
over the far horizon
through the dark trees
trumpets blaring
new flags unfurling
suddenly appearing
the closed ranks coming on
to the now-loud drums
the triumphant trumpets
brass horns and hollow bassos
ringing out
over the casqued warriors
the masked legionnaires
over the flashing columns
coming on and on
rank on rank
in new strange uniforms
no one has ever seen

VI

A consumer society consuming itself
dedicated to the pursuit of pleasure
is another way Caligula
might have put it
Life not something to be defeated
but to be consummated
like a marriage
of good and evil
or pleasure and pain
mixed with the sound of low singing
sweet melodies and prayers
And then the sound
              of hi-fi speakers
    which will bring
                  Vivaldi to St. Peter's
            in the loud spring—
                      Vivaldi to Il Papa
            Vivaldi Vaticano
                  Vox populi in Vivaldi
                  Il Papa Vivaldi—
                          in the Piazza San Pietro
    fifty thousand *turisti*
                      filling the holy horseshoe
            between the semicircle colonnades
    on the black cobbles and grey marble
                      the pilgrims pushing forward
        policed by Swiss Guards
                          beneath the great arches
        with the great standing statues on them
                heroic
                    high above
                        gesturing
            to the pilgrims thronging in

                                        by tour buses
                        grimy city autobuses
            Walking
                    limping
                            running
                                    the young lilting along
                                        with backpacks
                        the old crawling by
                        in black shawls
                            Friars and Anglican parishioners
                            pacing the colonnades
Fat nuns with moustaches and thick fingers
    hooded monks & mendicants
                        priests in shovel shoes
        Cappuccini
                        Franciscans
                                    Carmelites and rabbis
            scarlet bishops
                            elegant monsignors
        Tipsy French Cistercians
                and French sisters with fancy handbags
Moroccans in fezes with huge crucifixes
        Desert fathers come to town
                                sand between their toes
        Troops of Sicilian children
                bands of Greek boy scouts with banners
U.S. soldiers and sailors on USO tours
                St. Stanislaus ladies from Greenpoint Brooklyn
                bearing huge banners proclaiming
                                Greenpoint Lives!
The polyglot populi presses forward
                                under the hot sun
                toward Paulus the Pope
                            Giovanni Paulus il Secondo
who enters not through great doors flung open
                                on a high balcony

but in a big white jeep
with three cardinals in crimson beanies
And he in gleaming white
driven very slowly over the cobblestones
through the thousands
pressing on him
And Vivaldi's *Four Seasons* pouring forth
lilting and stately
filling the piazza
a hollow shell
echoing
Vivaldi fills the lighted air
swells the lighted air
takes wing and lifts
the ugly old
and young and fair
Too late and not too late
If God in spite of all
by some strange chance
exists

B y the beach at Ostia
      in an abandoned hotel
      like an empty ocean liner
we look out upon
      cabañas and beach umbrellas
   against hazy ocean
Mare Mediterraneo
     like a stage backdrop
  the perspective
     foreshortened
  the whole panorama
      seen through a wide-angle lens
  figures on high-dive platforms
       above the pools
    looking larger than life
     against the white sky
    standing heroic
      looking out
    And prone bodies
      in full sun
     laid out like corpses
      afloat on the hot sand
  All as in a scene
     from *Le Voyeur*
And far cries fade
Tattered shreds of voices
reach to us across the traffic
where we sit upon a balcony
     in shade

VIII

On the beach at Ostia
at Castelporziano
soft Roman spring now come and gone
the fierce summer sun
opens its furnace
Black sand and blown waves
schools of mackerel clouds
swimming through the sky
over far fishers at sea
trolling with outriggers
And on the black beach
fat ladies leading pasta husbands
hips and breasts sprung loose
with promise of pneumatic bliss
And pudgy bambinos
bandy-legged and drooling
on leather leashes tied to mamas
bawling at the sea

And the sea roars back
its lost answer

IX

The beach umbrellas like folded flowers
drooped in the dusk
by the abandoned cabañas
empty sands stretching away
Everyone swum away
over the hills of the sea
A hound trots by
looking for his master
turns his head to the sea
scents the heady air
as a red bird flies over
On the horizon the great ships
square sails raised in ancient wind
colored lateens and longboats
with banks of rowers
setting their sails and courses
on the turning tide
un riflusso rosso
Water pours off the beachheads
The film flows backward
to the first morning

Light upon the mountains
flows from the fountains

X

At Ostia Seaplane Basin
by the soccer field
by the trash heaps
by the empty lots and broken buildings
by the dark stone bench
by the three bare saplings

wind stirs a hand of dust

the dust of one *ragazzo di vita*
who fell here
where we stand
with reporters and *paparazzi*
wanting to know what we think
of the murder here
of one Pier Paolo Pasolini

Aie! Aie!
A voice beyond the world
screams retribution
for all the poets of the world
who fell here with him

XI

So came upon my self

in that darkest place

where lay the golden bough

upon that shadowed ground

And saw myself awaking there

as in a mirror made of air

And saw how self still tried

to rise from there

and fly as spirit should

and fly as spirit could

Through the dark wood

CANTI TOSCANI

I

Tuscan woman with olive eyes
            (the whites milk white)
    catches the last sun in them
      and flashes back the light
Pale lamps, in the night

II

Red sun setting
        over Toscana
through the cypresses
          over the red tile roofs
            and green lush vineyards
near Volterra and Piccioli
       Paesani on old bikes
         on straight dirt roads
and the trees turning brown
          like a drought
    as the sun goes out
and the streetlights
        coming on
          in little Ponsaco
  its iron churchbell clanging—

Night falls!

III

Toulouse-Lautrec of Lucca
                         by the Romanesque cathedral
        selling his Sunday paintings
                                    of the Duomo
            stands only four feet high
                            his hands full of sighs

IV

Sun of Lucca turning brown
                         like a ripe olive
        in olive-oil sky
                            drops its stone pit
                over the rim
                                of the town
                as olive light
                            floods the landscape

V

Tower of Pisa
        leans away from the sun
    which turns dark red
            as its day's work
                is done
and then falls down
           on the red tile roofs
  and pulls them down
        and pulls down the town
             into darkness
Only the tower stands up
          as night fills
              my cup

VI

Driving into Florence from the West
From the freeway through
the flashing cars and new
high room apartments
and glass houses
to the old city
by the old Arno
with its old bridges
We
    very gradually
                 re-
                   con-
                     struct
                       our
                           old old
                    illusions

CARRARA, LOOKING SEAWARD

Saw Carrara's marble mountains
   their great white faces
     open to the sea
Somewhere a voice was singing
               in sea caves off Saranza
    somewhere
             upon the white wind echoing
     far off
        in white stone sky
      Again . . .
              again . . .
                   still echoing
        voce delirante
              figlia di mare
       Breasts of white marble
             Hair blown back
     aie
      aie
        che tanta bella luce
        della carne umana

FABLE OF THE SO-CALLED BIRDS

A Picaresque Imbecility

In Rome
a woman goes to the powder room
and puts on another face
When she comes out
her husband does not know her
and takes her for a famous movie director
and takes her to the top
of the town of Spoleto
where they rent a room in an aviary
and proceed to take off
each other's feathers
And he's a red bird and she's a blue bird
but without their feathers they look alike
When they have finished
they take their feathers
and put them together in a big pillow
which they sleep on together
and in the morning
try to separate their feathers
Then they walk out into the Piazza del Duomo
where they are immediately captured naked
by the town birdcatcher
who runs with them to the Prince of the town
claiming they are twin love birds
from the Garden of Eden
who had to paste on feathers
so they wouldn't be taken
for Adam and Eve
But they are taken only for naked birds
who shouldn't be wandering around
without their feathers

and the polizia start chasing them
all over Italia
since it is against the law of gravity
for birds to go around without feathers
And so they run all over Umbria
with the polizia chasing them
with bags of feathers and pots of glue
And St. Francis has no sight of them
as they run past Assisi
but this is a fable
and Umbria a Communist district
and so when all the other wild animals
see what is happening to the two naked birds
with the polizia pursuing them
they call a Congress of Birds in Perugia
and vote to form a Union of Unfeathered Birds
and some red geese from Castiglione del Lago
offer their own lakeside nests
to the two naked birds
And so they settle down there
in the Commune di Castiglione del Lago
And Christ who was hung up crucified
in the local church on the main street
just as He is hung up
in every church around the world
comes down to the lake
and throws the nails from His hands
into the lake
and strokes the two birds with His bleeding hands
And His hands are healed
and He says Thank You and walks away over a hill
carrying His cross again
as if nothing had ever happened
but the two naked birds fish His nails
out of the lake and take them

to the Union of Shoemakers in town
and the shoemakers are so grateful
for these magic nails
that they give the two birds jobs as apprentices
And in this little shoe shop
the master cobbler has a pair of black birds
whom he has trained to pick up nails
and bring them to him one at a time
as he needs them
but while they are bringing the nails
they begin whispering in the ears
of the two naked birds
whispering to them that they too
had once been free birds
but that now they were enslaved
'just like workers everywhere'
because now that they had shoes
they wanted socks
and when they got socks
they wanted pants and shirts
and when they had them
they wanted coats and hats and brassieres
and nylons and neckties and houses and jewelry
and fur coats and sports cars
and everything they wanted they
would have to pay for
they would have to work for
and it was a capitalist plot
to enslave all workers everywhere
And the two crows paint such a horrible picture
of the capitalist consumer world
that the two naked birds
throw off their new shoes
and run over the horizon to Siena
where they run into a very strange bird indeed

who claims he can make feathers grow again
all over them
if they would only join
the Mystic Feather & Hairgrowers Union
but at this very moment in Siena
in the great shell-shaped Piazza
the natives are running the big horse race
the Palio
in which all the neighborhoods of Siena
compete with each other
and each district has one horse
and they each have their banner and their colors
and they race around the stone Piazza
at neckbreak speeds waving their banners
And now the district called Owl
wins the race
because the mascot owl
is riding on the head of the horse
and telling it how to run wisely
And when the naked birds
see the wise owl winning
with all its feathers on
and the prize wreath around its neck
they go running up to the owl
and ask him
how he remains so free and swift
and yet manages to retain all his feathers
And the owl nods his head without answering
and in the process of nodding his head
falls sound asleep
And in his sleep he hears himself hooting
And they hear him hooting that night
when they are sleeping
And it is a bad sign
the sound of him at night is a bad sign

a sign that something bad
is going to happen to you
And so the next day they get up very early
and run away again
to San Gimignano
the town of many towers on a hill
over a valley of vineyards
And they run through the valley at sunset
and reach San Gimignano
just as the swallows and pigeons
rise up to the tops of the trees and towers
to sing to the setting sun
And they too try to fly
to the tops of the towers
which were built by powerful families
each trying to prove
it was greater than the other
And the two naked birds realize
they cannot ever fly high enough
unless they grow real feathers again
and accept their natural condition again
but this they cannot do
because once the feathers are plucked
they do not grow back like hair
and it is like losing their virginity
in the Garden of Eden
and they can never fly purely again
And so they give it all up
and crawl back to Rome in the night
And take up Science
and learn aerodynamics and invent rocketry
and migrate to the United States of America
and give up Communism
and join the Space Program
and shoot off in a rocket to the moon

and fall back to earth
and try always to fly
to still higher and higher places
but always fall back to earth with parachutes
And as they fall they hear
way below and far away
the so-various singing of small free birds
hidden in green hills
in a garden called Love
in a district no longer shown on maps
and no longer represented
in the national legislature.

MILANO-BRUXELLES

Lost train shunted
through the Simplon Tunnel
as through a telescope
and out through the white peaks
and on out over the burnt landscape
Westward and North to the lowlands—
Nederland underland
An image of decadent Europe
flashed upon the train window
Land like old Camembert
bent houses, roofs like crusts
crenelated battlements
auto gravings rusty sidings
freight cars from five countries
run together
fleurs de fer fanées
But also the so-lush fields
deep lime-green meadows
full of huge brown cows
great rows of poplars blown
over the horizon
small farms in the deep bosque
And the stolid Belges descending at Mons
red cheeks and *bouches gonflées*
portmanteaux full of pork

AT THE *GARE BRUXELLES-MIDI*

Two people saying goodbye
but not saying it
Saying nothing
in the station at noon
in the *gare Bruxelles-Midi*
Not a word between them
They're both looking straight ahead
Their hands are clasped
on the cafe table
all four hands together
as in a children's hand game
Their hands are big
The man and the woman are not so big
They are grey and green
middle-aged
nondescript but distinguished
Even their skins seem grey
Il a l'air d'un petit fonctionnaire
a little bureaucrat somewhere
It is he who is taking the train
perhaps back to his wife in France
The woman here is a little younger
but far from young
Maybe he's French she's Belge
a wartime romance perhaps
Now forty years after
they're still meeting
across borders
Their four hands like the four wings of two doves
folded together
unable to fly away
from each other

Very capable hands
capable of a lot of things
but not of saying goodbye
not even of waving goodbye
Their hands are mute as mouths
He stands up now
He picks up
his heavy valise
He stands there still
She does not look up
He keeps standing there
looking nowhere
Then he walks away
All at once he walks away
around the corner out of sight
carrying his heavy valise
and his heavy briefcase
She does not look after him
She does not turn her head
She stares straight ahead
without blinking

A fly
walks
around
on the
table

TWO AMSTERDAMS

A voyage through the Low Countries
and tilted Amsterdam
like a barge in a bottle
a blown glass city
listing on its tides—
In the hotel café
they have rugs on the table
Dutch burghers munching mutton
while I sit here longing
         for the Transsiberian Express
      the wild taiga
          beyond Zima Station
  And the wide open spaces
          between Ship Rock and Taos
   high flat mesas like islands
          or ships adrift
            in the desert
        Indians in undented
          black felt hats
  And prairies in sun
       seas of wheat in wind
          off the Great Lakes
  Or the running sea
        sweeping in
          off Cape Ann Gloucester
  Or the wild North Sea
         due North of here
       Vikings beating windward
          through the white nights
    Norwegians in open boats
         escaping the Nazis
No more macho heroes here

among the potted rubber plants!
Yet not far away
throw-away heroes rocking onstage
at Paradiso dance hall
Amsterdam Fillmore Auditorium
stoned captain at the helm
with stand-up mike swung like a sword
to the sound of sea crashing
on splintered timber
The deck quivers
to the boomed electric beat
The ship tilts
the crew roars
in Liverpool accents
the naked hero-bodies crash
beyond the Milky Way
And in the blown-out dawn
nudes struggle home
through alleyways

THE LIVING THEATRE

In a little side street
off the Museumplein
a lady talking on a telephone and crying
and staring out her secondfloor window
looks through me in the street

A block further on
a man looking down and smoking
and laughing in his telephone
looks through me invisible

The ground of the Ruksmuseum Park
is covered with sodden leaves
My footsteps
will leave no prints on them
But they and the people have left
their imprints in me
their distant emotions
fall on me as in
some tragic magic theatre

I do not laugh and cry with them
I am just their dramaturge
or some foreign theatre critic
come to see the spectacle
of their little lives played out

This show will never fold
no matter what the reviews
Tragedies will be tragedies
even if they laugh
The human comedy will still be comedy

even if not laughable
The show will go on
even if it's not Paradise Now
in the Living Theatre

HORSE IN AMSTERDAM,
AFTER REMBRANDT

If I could read the blazed face

of this huge horse at night

with its hair like black flame

and its eyes charred chestnuts

I would want for words to tell

of the deeps drowned there

and the dumb world muted there

where the souls of dark trees

raise their raving arms

And nothing stops the stoned night

in the wilderness of its eyes

A NOTE AFTER READING THE DIARIES
OF PAUL KLEE

Paul Klee (that painter who never could draw very well)
put on the holes in his socks
on those dim mornings when he woke alone
On other days it was a different tale
as after that time they made love
in the larch grove
by the Tegernsee

What perfection we reach with love!
he opined
It even knits up socks
and makes me feel I'm God in humankind
(Blow, blow, thou winter wind!
Crumble, ye mountains of the mind!)

American River College Library

EXPRESSIONIST HISTORY
OF GERMAN EXPRESSIONISM

The Blue Rider rode over The Bridge into the Bauhaus
on more than one blue horse
Franz Marc made his blue mark
on the blue scene
And Kirchner cantered through the dark circus
on a different dark horse
Emil Nolde never moldy danced boldly
around a golden calf
Max Pechstein fished in river landscapes
and fooled around with his models
(They all did that)
Rottluff painted his rusty lust
and Otto Mueller ate cruellers
as his painting got crueler
Erich Heckel heckled himself with madmen
and thereby foresaw their mad ends
Norwegian Munch let out a silent scream
Jawlensky made Matisse look mad and Russian
And Kandinsky grew insanely
incandescent
Kokoschka drew his own *sturm und drang*
Käthe Kollwitz chalked the face
of Death and the Mother
Schwitters twittered through trash cities
and Klee became a clay mobile
swaying to the strains of the Blue Angel
Otto Dix drew a dying warrior
on his steely palette
Grosz glimpsed the grossest
in the gathering storm
Max Beckmann saw the sinking of the Titanic

and Meidner painted the Apocalypse
Feininger traced a Tragic Being
and fingered skyscrapers
which fell across the Atlantic
(and the Bauhaus in its final antic
fell on Chicago)
Meanwhile back in Berlin
Hitler was painting himself
into a corner
And his ovens were heating
as a Tin Drum began beating

THE REVOLUTIONARY

Like a blind one at the frontiers
Far from Vorovsky Street
Far from the street of Kropotkin
Long after Pasternak and Lara
A blind flame springs up
Far from the street of Kropotkin
a blind fire burns
in the heart of crystal
like the flame in the heart of a flower
like a broken blade in a stone
like the broken light in fields of wheat
Far from the street of Kropotkin
like a lantern swung in the high wind
that swept the snow
that covered the stars of blood
in the street of Kropotkin

Her eyes aflame in his heart

THE PHOTO OF EMILY

She wore a cloche hat
She was Aunt Emily
She spoke French She had a job
as a French governess
She stood on the bridge in Bronxville
over the Bronx River the little river
with its little woods and the little bridge
and the swimming hole and the woods
where we played Robin Hood
I thought I was Robin Hood
or one of his deerskin men
I wanted a deerskin suit
more than anything
I remember that clearly when I was eight
I stayed awake at night
thinking how to make it how to get it
I would have robbed a rich traveller
(That's how rebels are born)
She stood on the bridge in her hat
I came to her from the woods
where I'd been playing
by the little brown river
with its dirty crayfish
I came up to her
in her long lace dress and black pumps
She had elegant feet
long feet
an 'aristocrat's' she would say
She was a bit mad and elegant
Even then I knew it
She was Catholic in a mad way
as if she had some special personal connection

with the Pope
She thought of herself as a writer
as having something special to say
in French
I thought of her as my French mother
She was my mother's French sister
the sister who'd been born in France
the family so mixed up
between Portugal and France
and the Virgin Islands
which was the route my mother's family took
to the United States
and Coney Island where the French kept
boardinghouses
and my mother met my father
when he came from Lombardy
speaking only Lombard
and ended up the first night
in that boardinghouse at Coney
My French mother Emily stands on the bridge
in the old photo
the only photo I had of her
A dark bridge and her face in shadow
Or perhaps her face was light once
and the photo darkened
There is a pearly strangeness
in the dark light
It is all I have of her
She must have had a box camera that day
I was wearing short pants
on that little stone bridge
(And who took the picture
of the two of us together
arms around each other?
So silent the old picture—

If it could only speak!)
It is her day off in the Nineteen Twenties
I am nine—
Where now
that elegant cloche hat
that woman lost in time
a shadowy strangeness is all
She had fine skin
gossamer hair
cut like Garbo
or Louise Brooks
but not so beautiful
She had a wen on her breast
Might I not find that hat
and that woman still—
a seamstress in the back
of some small thrift shop—
Come back, come back—
At least the photo
might I not at least
find the photo again
in some lost album
with black cardboard pages
there's the photo
held on the stiff page
by little paper triangles pasted on
the photo of Emily
mad and elegant
thinking herself a great writer
with something to say to the world
in her shadow hat
having her picture taken
with the child she always wanted
She had lovers but no child
She stood by the bedside and took me

Life went on with us
The photo darkened
She was too distracted
too gypsy-like too self-willed
too obsessed too
passionately articulate
burning too bright
too much a lunatic of loving
to keep that child
who ran off finally
into the dark park of those days
by the Bronx River
and sees her now
nowhere else in memory
except by that dark bridge
And saw her never again
And never saw her again
except in the back of old boutiques
peered into now again
with haunting glance
in the Rue de Seine

LATE IMPRESSIONIST DREAM

In a late Impressionist dream I am riding in an open touring-car with a group of French women in summer dresses and picture hats with uncles in grey doeskin vests and striped shirts with armbands and everyone is laughing and chattering in French as if no other language had yet become socially accepted And we get to an outdoor cafe by the Seine on the outskirts of Paris as in a Manet painting under an arbor by the river drinking wine and eating a grand picnic out of wicker hampers And at the next table a group of French intellectuals are indulging in their famous *grande logique* proving that such-and-such is really an oxymoron And just then some loud young men drift by in punts on the river looking sheepishly like young American college students singing a drinking song about Whiffenpoofs and we go on talking French as if nothing else in the real world were happening anywhere And all the people around me turn into characters out of Marcel Proust and we are all in Swann's Way in a budding grove with a straight Odette chez Swann but then of a sudden Blaise Cendrars bursts in waving a newspaper headline screaming *"L'OR! L'OR!"* and gold has been discovered in California and I must leave immediately to join the Gold Rush and wake up in my cabin in Big Sur looking like a French Canuck Jack Kerouac and hearing the sound of the sea in which the fish still speak Breton

PLANE LIFE

TWA to Boston and
a woman in 'Ambassador' Class having a
heart attack while the
passengers wearing headphones are all
laughing hilarious at
a movie with
Dustin Hoffman in
which he
impersonates a woman and
they bring in the oxygen tank and
pump her up and
when she comes to she
starts crying and moaning over and over
Oh I am going to die
I am going to die
And the passengers all still roaring
the woman weeping and moaning
I am going to die!
but

She doesn't
The movie continues
The laughers continue
The plane like life itself
sails on
carrying its helpless
passengers

INSCRUTABLE

Flying blind from Paris
at forty thousand feet

the lonely roads of Nova Scotia
wandered far below

clouds clustered like blossoms
stuck to the land—

Where now, all you wandering cars and people,
dumb animals, ants, far below,
your truths still hidden,
blind in your courses?

Unreadable faces in the plane,
indecipherable palms of hands,
unreadable maps of living,
inscrutable life, face of time,
still shrouded in your mystery!

THE PLOUGH OF TIME

Night closed my windows and
The sky became a crystal house
The crystal windows glowed
The moon
shown through them
through the whole house of crystal
A single star beamed down
its crystal cable
and drew a plough through the earth
unearthing bodies clasped together
couples embracing
around the earth
They clung together everywhere
emitting small cries
that did not reach the stars
The crystal earth turned
and the bodies with it
And the sky did not turn
nor the stars with it
The stars remained fixed
each with its crystal cable
beamed to earth
each attached to the immense plow
furrowing our lives

THE REBELS

Star-stricken still
   we lie under them
      in dome of night
  as they wheel about
     in their revolutions
   forming and reforming
        (oh not for us!)
    their splendiferous
      phosphor fabrications

Ah the wheelwright of it
      (whoever he or she or it)
   chief fabricator
     of the night of it
    of the night to set it in
      this cut-glass
       diamond diagram

Upstairs
  in the lighted attic
    under the burning eaves
       of time
  lamps hung out
   (to guide far more far-out voyagers
    than ourselves)

Still antic stars
    shoot out
     burst out—
       errant rebels
     even there
   in the perfect pattern

                    of some utopia
            shooting up
                        tearing the
                                silver web
            of perfect symmetry

As in a palm of hand
            the perfect plan of line
                        of life and heart and head
        struck across of a sudden
                        by one
                                cataclysmic tear

Yet all not asunder
                all not lost to darkness
        all held together still
                    at some still center
                even now
            in the almost incendiary dawn
        as still another
                    rebel burning bright
                        strikes its match upon
                                our night

HISTORY OF THE WORLD:
A TV DOCU-DRAMA

Now humanity does not know where to go,
because no one is waiting for it: not
even God. —Antonio Porchia

Dark mind dark soul dark age
the peasant leads his horse
through blackberry kingdoms
and comes out at a crossroads
in North America
comes out on a highway
in the American West
the horse hitched to a prairie wagon
the ruts get wider
East of Santa Fe you can see from a plane
the old wagon trails in the earth
ruts a mile wide
you can almost hear
the crack of whips over horses
the cries of the drivers in the rising dust
The nineteenth century ends
and turns into Highway 66
prairie schooners into Pullmans
their dark saloons sheeted in oblivion
The myth haunts us
the rutting continues
The night of the horse is over
It is the dawn after dreaming
in the great American night
in the middle of the journey
we come upon our selves on a dark road
and recognize our selves for the first time

The lights come on
the country is electrified
the world lights up like a ferris wheel
All the machines begin to hum
almost in unison
Europa become a blind bull
hitched to an iron horse on rails
belching smoke
Civilization beats out Eros
and Proust perishes
Gauguin escapes to Tahiti
as Tristes Tropiques
perish forever
A crowd flows over London Bridge
Westward
stick figures in the world's end
out of Giacometti
The Golden Hinde sails through the Golden Gate
and sets up as a tourist attraction
Sir Francis Drake's brass plate is dug up
and ends up in a glass case
in Bancroft Library Berkeley
The Tower of London is sold
and transported to Texas
Easy Riders over the asphalt
roar stoned into the sunset
Stout Cortez still astounded on a peak
A Passage to India
and an empire collapses
as Spengler shouts 'I told you so!'
Chinese philosophers dreaming they are butterflies
drift up the Yangtse and disappear
as the sea continues its blind waves
Red tides reach up the Potomac
and paranoia floods the world

116

Drums drums drums Johnny Get Your Gun
In the morning still
a girl in a white linen dress
wearing a white picture hat
crosses Gatsby's lawn bright with promise
Gandhi dies but lives on
A Buddhist monk
immolates himself on-camera
Sri Ram Jai Ram Jai Jai Ram
Jesus on his Tree sticks up
on his horizon
signalling wildly
The rutting continues
'Strengthened to live Strengthened to die
for medals and positioned victories?'
'The world's an orphan's home'
Rootless polyglots roam the cities
spacecraft sweeping over
bearing short-haired Magellans in jumpsuits
as satellites sweep the earth
with high-resolution cameras
multiple fluid images
melding Minneapolis and Roumania
Mississippi and Krishna
Hari rama hari rama Rama rama hari hari
Fields and winds and waters
fog and birds and men
sweep the screen
and chase each other from it
The camera zooms in:
The Vietnam captain holds his pistol
to the peasant's head
It explodes in full color
on CBS ABC NBC
The world with its drums of blood

continues turning
The locust continues
to devour the world
Hunger persists
Love lurches on
listing to larboard
like a ship in a bottle
Human longing goes on
Loneliness a curse
Innocence persists
Ignorance persists
like a scratch on a TV window
like a scratch on a windshield
Twilight has no meaning
beyond the figurative
Europa rocks on the horizon
lights burning in the night
like the SS Queen Mary
tied up in Southern California
where the American Dream came too true
There is a soughing in the bilges
Somewhere a naive figure
holds up a laurel wreath
a nymph a valkyrie a sybil
holds up a Golden Bough
Lovers still are riders to the sea
A horse comes alone from a torn village
Ah love let us be true
to our selves
I'll put a note in a bottle
like a schooner in a bottle
it'll survive the worst seas
the holocaust will be hollow
Turner's shipwreck burning
off the Hook of Holland

Friend, an albatross wings above our land
It's a bird It's a man It's a plane without wings
'Brightness falls from the air'
and the air burns
They used to call it a Darkling Plain
In the UN they are debating it
'It's still the same old story
a fight for love and glory'
A woman walks on the shore
Life still an inn of joy and sorrow
Beloved come back
by any bridge
Educated armies
march over it
In the twilight holding up her skirts
Anna Livia stands
on the far strand at ebb-tide
'swept with confused alarms'
An effect of Rembrandt
an effect of Turner
The air is shaken with light
the crickets begin again
on heavy summer nights
Somewhere in the snows
someone is beating a woman
A Russian poet records it
Boots begin
to march over it
The camera zooms in:
All the windows in every house in the world
turn into TV screens
all tuned to the same image
the image of children watching and waiting
watching a huge strange drifting cloud
Children are watching children waiting

The great cloud drifts ever closer and brighter
shaking the screen with shattered light
the broken light of modern painting
an effect of Jackson Pollock of Franz Kline of DeKooning
There's Nothing on the other channels
There's no sound
A child reaches up and turns up the volume
Still there's no sound
still there's only silence
still there's only the Ultimate Stillness
A child turns up the Brightness

INDEX

PS 3511 .E557 O9 1988
Ferlinghetti, Lawrence.
European poems & transitions

122